THE SMELL OF BLOOD

K. STEWART

iUniverse, Inc.
New York   Bloomington

The Smell of Blood

iUniverse books may be ordered through booksellers or by contacting:

iUniverse
1663 Liberty Drive
Bloomington, IN 47403
www.iuniverse.com
1-800-Authors (1-800-288-4677)

ISBN: 978-0-595-49331-9 (pbk)
ISBN: 978-0-595-61058-7 (ebk)

Printed in the United States of America

iUniverse rev. date: 5/7/2009

CONTENTS

THIS BOOK IS DEDICATED TO MY SONS AND THEIR CHILDREN IN THE HOPE THAT THEY WILL NEVER HAVE TO GO TO WAR AND TO JASMINE FOR HER HELP IN SO MANY WAYS.

MY OLYMPICS

My Olympics were in a hot
dirty
wild place called Vietnam.

The crowds were screaming monkeys
screeching insects
and vegetable indifference.

The judging was hostile
severe
and final as death.

The swimming event was through your own sweat
and the monsoon rain
sometimes through mud
somewhere between quicksand
and cold lava
an event that took awhile to get into.

There was no quitting until it was done.

I did poorly in leech wrestling
but made up for it in mosquito swarming and feeding.

My high jumps left me doing psychedelic somersaults
in a kaleidoscope of tracers
flashes and explosions of red and white.

I failed to place in ear removal.
I admit I didn't adequately train for the event
but I did excel in jungle dash
and hurdles.

A 12 minute dash through hundreds of pissed-off, armed men
hostile
and sending bullets like deathly clouds
of sleet through the air

the first man dead before he hit the ground.

My steeplechase was a six day run
through the jungle
chased by dogs and 500 vampires
all hungry for blood
to survive in a fiery finish
with the thumping applause of bullets
passing through helicopter skin.

The groupies were young
cheap, dirty and at least infected
not readily impressed by a two mile dash
through jungle and shrapnel.

The awards and medals were corrupted
some very deserving mixed
with those of politics and lies.

The ultimate judgment
survival
some by luck
some by skill
some by karma
but all wounded, stained
and forgotten after the closing ceremony.

ESCAPE VELOCITY

I carry all kinds of baggage
some obvious
and some so profoundly subtle

like a creeping neurotoxin
claiming your power of ambulation
speech
and then your soul.

An old friend mentioned
he'd rarely seen me really smile.
I was surprised.
Am I unhappy
a sorrowful soul and being?
Is my happiness and smile so rare?
How can this be?
Why?

Then, I have to admit
it is a war wound.
I'm scarred
and limping through life.

I don't deserve to be too happy
because I'm shamed and blamed.

I wasn't valiant
a holy warrior.
God wasn't on my side.
God wasn't even there.
He left the mess
to lesser deities
rage, hate
greed, lust
and other base passions
for the lost and desperate.

I became addicted to the rush
of death and desperation
of living on the sharp divide
between surviving and being alive
or unfortunate and dead.

The capricious roll of the dice
fate
or God's will.

If I keep moving fast enough
maybe I can reach escape velocity
and break the bonds of gravity
and my shame.

If I had only been more sure
more capable
more something.

If I could change the past
who knows if I wouldn't just fuck it up
some other way.

But I can't change the past
no second chance.
You can look at it
wonder about it
name it
blame it
hate it
or wish it wasn't
but you can't change it.

Maybe
just maybe
I can still run fast enough
to run right past it.
Fast enough to tear away the shame
fast enough to leave the past behind
fast enough to reach the future
to stop running

sit down
and smile.

Some Thursday   1967

Christopher,
These are the lonely days. The hollow time. Near the end. Dreams
of fantasy. Fears of dissolution.   A shaky hand from fluids I drink.
Impotent music. Fearful minutes I live these days.
Wind spitting on my face
tearing clothes around my body
flinging limbs about my ears
puddles clapping
as I am walking
Product of a sterile mind.   Where was I during the castration?
Already nearing sleep. I have been ill lately. But the coming and
the leaving are all the same. The living is the energy -- the plea-
sure. The illusion. Wheezing, falling, smiling, mumbling at the sun.
Shelter stray treasures you may find.
Ken

JUNGLE SMELL

In the jungle
we would go unbathed
no smokes
no soap in our clothes
nothing
to raise our scent
like an alarm
through the bushes

it wasn't dogs
we were afraid of
but a human nose

just walking slowly
silently
for a long time

dancing along the hormone tightrope
senses become keen
and even a smoker's nose
can read the breeze

catch a hint of smoke
hundreds of yards away
in thick, triple canopy jungle

smell another human's body
almost as far

smell the weather
animals
fear

moving slowly
silently
and sniffing
also listening carefully

for the jungle is filled
with so much noise
the only telltale sign
was a patch of silence

my ears
were never quiet
the constant buzz
of too many rounds
and explosions, too close

and seeing
was limited at times
to less distance
than covered if you fell down

that just left
the nose
and smell

after a while
my sense of smell
was so good
I could smell the future

smell
spilled blood before its time

first
I thought
it was an olfactory hallucination
an unusual weed
that when wet
gave off the scent
of sticky, hot, fresh
blood

after enough encounters
I had to accept it
for what it was
the steamy, hot sweet

smell
of fresh spilled blood
but I never could tell
whose

the first few minutes
out the door
and on the ground
quickly away from
the aviation fuel exhaust

in the bush
a couple of quick sniffs
and if I smelled that smell
I knew
someone's blood would run
and I couldn't tell whose

it may have been minutes
it may have been days

before we rode the helicopter back
somebody
left a donation
for mother earth
a most likely unintentional
gift of nitrogen

it had me too paranoid
to appreciate the significance
of the power to smell
not only over great distances
but through time

in comparison
my efforts to smell my world
seem so mundane
so wasteful
like dogs able to track
a faint human scent
deriving their greatest joy

burying their noses into each other's
musk

aromatic time travel
how does science account
for that

it doesn't fit
our basement bondage
views of the laws
of physics and matter

maybe you could
smell trouble
or good fortune
like you could feel
someone looking at you

maybe
you could smell
right from wrong

smell the past

it could help us
get through the present

snorting time riders
of the purple sage
possibly a new group

smell your past lives
sniff out your true path
sit down and smell
who you really are

VETERAN BLUES

Is this the fate
of aging veterans
to be holding back
the tears
at the pathetically
romantic ending
of a bad war book?

The blissful
idealized
dream-life
you dreamed
when you
were at war.

The camaraderie
of young men
brothers in arms
undergoing
heinous trial
and tribulation
supporting each other
and in man-love
struggling against
the common foe.

After fighting
long and hard
overcoming
incredible odds
killing so many
professionally
with a unique flair
a special few
return home
to a wonderful job.

Interesting
but not too exciting
with a beautiful
loving
totally supportive wife.

Who
somehow
innately knows
who you really are
what you really need
and how wonderful
you really can be.

Even though
you're repressed
jacked up
hostile
and self-involved.

A couple of special lines
reaffirming
the validation
of so many
young men's deaths.

They may not have
"died for a cause"
but for sure
"they died for each other."

Holy bullshit
it hurts
that the illusions
and fantasies
can still cause pain

pain
without gain.

What I remember

is the
loneliness.

The aching loneliness
begat by fear
in a young man's heart
and no one else
to really share
that fear with.

Not allowed
to be afraid
and show it.

Not allowed
to admit
you're less than enthusiastic
or casual
about your own death.

Desperate
heart breaking
loneliness
drove me
to pitiful whorehouses.

Feeble
plywood shacks,
a single room
divided up
with flimsy curtains.
Five or more women
sharing
a common wash basin
on the floor
where one of them
would squat
splash water on
her crotch
and make

"sexy talk"
trying to attract
her next customer.

I would sit down
wait for friends
and just talk
with an occasional
woman
who was not too busy
or desperate
for money
right then.

The first people
I ever opened up to
however hesitantly,
were Vietnamese
prostitutes.

I would share
small parts of myself
that were boiling
in turmoil
under bondage
and repression
in my life.

It was like
trying
to pop a pimple,
to relieve a large
painful
boil
and gave me some relief.

Beginning
to know these people
the trash
of their society
the discarded

the forgotten
the unimportant
made it harder
to take the life
of another
Vietnamese.

Not at first.
At first
I wanted to lash out.

My anger fueled
by the mistreatment
of these hard working
struggling
women.

But, there I was
in the whorehouse.

The most beautiful woman
I'd ever seen
was Eurasian.

I met her
outside the barbed wire perimeter
of a special forces camp
on the Cambodian border.
A place called
Dak To,
where the 173rd Airborne brigade
was chewed up
in the mud and jungle
and I waded
through crotch high mud
and bodies
laid out like a lawn
in the woods.

This woman
had pale green eyes

fine
light olive skin
long, straight black hair
and a slender
well proportioned body.

She was beautiful
and for sale.

Three mama sans
were pimping her off
to the local boys.

I came to the wire
with my friends.

Being near death
had fired up my testosterone
like everybody else's.
A primal need
to copulate
and procreate
was strong
mindless
and almost overpowering.

All I could think of
was the story
"Cinderella."

Those mama sans
were purposefully
cruel
arrogantly disdainful
and malicious
in their treatment
of this young woman.

I was overtaken
by her presence
and was the first

to take her away
to a nearby hillside
where a poncho
was strung out
over four posts
about three feet
off the ground
and a filthy blanket
had been laid down
on the grass.

She took off her pants
pulled up her shirt
and laid down
still.

I was humbled
and overwhelmed.

A woman
whose only crime
was being half French
was magnificent in appearance
and somehow
self-possessed.
Now she was stretched out
as a sacrifice
to older women
who hated her.

My French was bad
my Vietnamese, worse
and she had no English.

How could I tell her
I just wanted
to know her
was incapable
of "fucking" her?

"Here's ten bucks,

just keep it.
I just wanted
to be with you
for a while.

I wanted to pretend
I could tell you
things.
That I somehow
find your presence here
amazing
encouraging
and horrible.

At the same time
I just wanted
to be with someone
to touch something
outside of myself."

I was willing
to pay the money for her time
that she needed
to show her
keepers
her masters.

But
she did not understand
gave me back the money
and put her pants back on.

Even from a distance
it was obvious
we weren't in the normal
position
for this kind of transaction.

When we walked back
my friends said
"What's the matter

couldn't get it up?"

So I said
"She wouldn't give me
a blowjob
and I got mad
and took my money back."
Continuing the game
that kept us all
in bondage.

Much later on
stoned
out of my mind
on NVA pot
confiscated
from a dead medic
I tried to touch this subject
with someone
who was the closest thing
to a friend
and said
"I just couldn't fuck her.
She was a person
that needed to be loved."

He said,
"No problem.
I have the same thing.
I just can't get into
these gook women
sometimes.
So I just think
about Carol back home.
What the hell
it's all the same
between the legs."

Took another toke
ate some more Red Cross candy
and never

talked about it again.

Looking back
I wish I'd had the courage
or the insight
to have done something
that made a difference.

Months later
I was near a small town
which was
off limits,
everyone restricted to base.

I snuck out
with only my Randall knife.
I was low
and needed to get some pot
to smoke.

I was with someone
who actually had some cash.

We scored from a couple
of street urchins
and were on our way back.

We passed a mama san
in a market,
a crinkly, shriveled up
ancient crone
screeching in a way
that Vietnamese
can be made unpleasant.

She was selling
a four year old
Amerasian child,
a pretty young girl,
for ten bucks.

This could have been
that other woman's beginnings.
What this child had
to look forward to
a life of pain
suffering
abuse
and no love.

I had no money
or the transaction
would have been quick
and over.

I had no rifle
to take the child
from this woman.

Hostile stares
all around
from other Vietnamese.

A group of men
paying too much attention
from the corner of a
nearby stall
pale, pasty Vietnamese
jungle trackers
and NVA for sure.

The scene was bad
bringing out
only a knife
wouldn't work.

I could take
this girl back
make her a bed
under mine at the rear
to watch
my stuff

while I was gone
and tell people
she was going to wash
my clothes
and make my bed.

Somehow
I'd be able to take her back
to America
to give her the chance
the opportunity
anybody deserves.

The pale men
were moving
too close.
My friend grabbed me.
"Let's split.
It's a bad scene,
let's get out of here."

We made a quick
retreat.
We made our escape.

Once on the shore
of the South China Sea
a place
called Tuy Hoa

after many months
of being shot at
and chased around
by more NVA
than you could
shake a stick at

trench foot
shriveled up
and leech digested,

we dropped our clothes
on the shore
and ran in like schoolboys into the sea.

Splashing around
having a good time.

When we came out
I noticed my wallet
was gone.

I screamed at a couple
of scrawny young boys
nearby
"Who stole my wallet?
I'm gonna kick your ass."

Right in their face
screaming at the top
of my lungs.

Innocent look
and trembling hands
they didn't know anything.
"Don't know
know nothing."

Naked
hairy, wet
big man
screeching at young
spindly kids.

A guy came over
and said
"Want your wallet back?
No problem."

He grabbed
the closest kid
took him immediately

into the surf
and held him under the water
turned to the other kids
and yelled
"Get his wallet, now!"

Seconds
ticked by.
The kid was thrashing.
Time stretched out
the kid moved less
and less.

I said
"Fuck this
get the kid out of there, man."

He said
"Ah just watch this."

The kid
was barely moving.

Suddenly
there was a flap
at my feet.
I looked down
there was my wallet.

The guy picked the kid
out of the water
and threw him on the shore
where he gasped
halfheartedly
for air.

The other kids
quickly picked him up
and half dragged him
back toward the

village.

"That's how you get
your wallet back
from these fuckers,"
said my friend.

At the time
I felt bad
that it bothered me
that he would take
a young child
and maybe kill him
for a piece of leather
couple pieces of plastic
and hardly any money.

Soon my time
was almost over
and I looked forward
so much
to leaving the madness.
Going back
to an American fantasy
still possible
to envision
in the middle 60s.

I'd paid my dues.
I was ready
to be rewarded.

That's part of the reason
I sit in a chair
reading a bad
overly romanticized
Vietnam war novel
and fight back the tears.

What we did
was not appreciated.

What we did
caused much pain
and suffering.

If what we did
served any purpose
it remains obscure to me
to this day.

I'm sad for our
innocence
sad
for all the innocents
and sad
that it goes on still
every day
somewhere.

DOUBT

Friends
dead
lost in blown away dreams
potential into nothing
after sharing space with you

it's scary
at first
it could have been you

you feel some relief
feel somehow
special
blessed
graced
and then
guilty

maybe somehow
you held back
in the fight
gave somewhat less
than you could

maybe showed less
than the proper enthusiasm
to struggle

maybe you let them
wave their red flag
in death's face
make more quick movements
to distract death
away from you

you can think about it
recall your heroic stances

remember clearly
your smooth capable
displays of competence
and daring

you know you didn't hold back
you fought a good fight
you know it's true
that it was just a matter
of bad luck
bad timing
or short timing karma
their karma

but the feeling creeps up
they died
not you

inside
you doubt
deeply doubt
your worth
your courage
and even your faith
and next time
you dance a little closer
to death
shake your mojo
loudly
and strut

more afraid of being afraid
than afraid

fire up the hormones
dance
the adrenaline rush
lost in the flow
of chemicals
you're just along
for the ride

the chemicals
that keep you up
and buffered
from more dead friends
more tattered bodies
until
the euphoria of survival
slowly
fades away
and you wonder
again

seek sense
or reason
in death's choices
seek meaning
in your survival

transiently comfortable
to have made it

happy
for sure
but still afraid
you may be cheating

cheating who
yourself
your friends
or death

death
and doubting
are "D" words
like dismal
depressed
destroyed
deranged
disenfranchised
disillusioned

disgusted
dismayed
detrimental
dastardly
deceived
dispossessed
and debauched

which leads us
to Drugs
a side trip

seeking that euphoric
comfort
of struggle

some work
sometime
somehow and in some way
but death
still brings
doubt

whether you feel
dejected
rejected
or neglected
just depends
on the timing
the space

when death looks straight
into your eyes
a stare
your soul can feel

nothing you do
to escape
can be anything less
than necessary

no more doubts
no more philosophical interpretations
no more wondering
of even the weather
and until death
is not distracted
heads straight
for your heart
you'd wonder
and doubt

it's amazing how quickly
that doubt can dissolve

just living
leaving the doubts
for another time
maybe tomorrow
not today

MEMORIAL BLUES

On memorial day
standing across
from the state cemetery
a flight of jets
roar overhead
in missing wing-man formation.
For some reason
it touches me.

Somehow
brings back a familiar
and distant ache
and I try to figure out
where it's coming from.

Does it bring people
blown away with time
and forgotten
or people who survived
and lived
and walked away from it all
but somehow not whole
leading me back?

Lost time
lost innocence
lost ambition
lost physical parts
and pieces of soul
somehow still tied
through many years,
many layers of memories
and events
to an invisible
incredibly strong
umbilical cord.

The smells, places
and death.
I'm following it back
through all that time.

I find it hard to remember
just what it is
that I am missing.

Was it the change
from a young man
to a grown man's life?
Was it the distant
remembered past
ambitions
wishes and delusions
not realized
or realized too much?

Is it the memory of things
done not quite right
things not done at all
missed opportunity
missed youth?
Am I just missing myself?

Is my younger self
judging who I am now?
Am I judging
who I was then?

Do I feel many eyes peering out
through distance
and jungle
darkness?
Looking at me
as if to say
"We didn't have the chance
and you did
and look what you have done."

Ghosts of youth robbed
young men dead
before they realized
what they had to lose
what they'd given up.

"Shit! you're alive Fool"
and their hopes and aspirations
lay heavy on my shoulders.

I start rummaging
through my bag of excuses
mitigating circumstances
microscopic
and brutal
injuries
scar tissue
the vagaries
of circumstance
and luck.

The eyes keep staring
and accepting no answers.

I'm still carrying
my heavy load.

Web gear sagged down
but no weapon
no grenades
no bullets
no right to kill
exiled
sad
in a land of memories.

DEATH

It was late at night,
but not late enough
that no one was up.
We were drinking beers,
smoking pot,
telling stories and lies.
I went outside to take a piss.
I undid my fly
and started to do my business.
I looked up and noticed
the moon.
It was huge
and blood red.
It was one of the most spectacular moons
I had ever seen,
blood red
and angry,
a perfect war moon.
Something strange was happening to it.
It took me awhile to realize
that there was an eclipse in progress.
The moon became ever more dark and angry red.
I shook off,
closed my fly,
yelled for people to come outside
and see this amazing wonder.
My friends piled out
in the same dazed state I was in.
There were a dozen or more of us
standing around in this magical moment.
The moon was darker, and darker
until it became fixed blood red
in the fullness of its eclipse.
The color was insane,
inflammatory,
insightful and damning.
The sky was pierced

and mortally wounded,
a large red hole in its body.
The moon and color inflamed our emotions.
We all began screaming,
hollering and yelling.
This screaming and yelling turned into incantations
and taunting.
Howling, chest beating,
screaming and flashing knives,
we were transformed into another world.
The world we lived in battle
and in our dreams.
We become possessed by spirits of the night
passion and death.
I raised my head
and started howling.
This moon had inspired me,
got the blood flowing,
got the juices moving.
What a powerful
primitive omen,
it affected us profoundly.
We were yelling,
carrying on,
screaming
and shouting into the sky.
The moon set off uncontrollable passions
in our hearts
and minds.
We were warriors
filled with blood lust
and empowered by our god
in the heavens.
As the angry moon encouraged
the war hormones to flow
I could feel them
cursing through my veins
and pounding through every muscle fiber
and bone.
I was invincible.
I was a warrior from the heavens.

I was inhumanly strong.
I was a monster of war.
I felt invulnerable
to any physical harm
or even death.
I began screaming out challenges.
I had danced with death
so many times
and come out victorious.
I had delivered
the death blows to others,
won the joust,
stood victorious
in the Coliseum of my war.
I began screaming obscenities at death.
I had become too powerful
for even its fingers to hold.
I became disrespectful
and taunting.
I had inspired the others.
We were screaming defiant challenges
to Death.
"You can't touch me.
You can't hold me.
There is no fear in my heart.
Fuck you
Death.
Fuck you to hell.
I would crush you
in my hands.
You're nothing before my power."
Like primal savages,
howling and screaming
driven insane
by the powerful moon.
I started singing
" Death, oh death
you've painted me with your blade.
Oh death, oh death
there is nothing new you can say.
Oh death,

we swam in your blood too long.
Oh death,
we know what you have done wrong.
You used us and abused us
as tools for your concern
and we hate the way you take all the credit
that we have earned.
Oh death, oh death,
leave our bones alone.
They are the ones that we earned,
the ones that we get to carry home."
Others started singing.
Screaming so loud in the power
of possession and transformation.
We were all consumed.
I began yelling,
"Fuck you death.
You don't scare me.
I looked into that face too many times to be afraid.
You're nothing to me.
I'm so bad that I can kill you!
I have faced hundreds
with too few bullets and a knife.
I have left my body because it was too slow
in combat to take other lives.
Fuck you death, you've got nothing on us.
You are nothing but a scavenger.
A crow, a hyena
and sometimes even a maggot.
You're just a terrible lie,
a pathetic fuck,
useless
and have nothing on us.
Nothing. Nothing."
We screamed at full volume,
past vocal control.
Jumping up and down,
swaying,
dancing in some pagan rhythm.

Where he came from,

when he appeared
I could not say,
but, there he stood,
tall
and unmoving
except for the blowing
of his large black cloak.
Black cloak and dark.
No, not black just no color,
a black hole in our vision.
Our incantations
had brought Death to us.
We were beyond caring.
Our blood was flowing hot
with our power and passion.
His cloak began to wave in a hot furnace wind
howling like the cries of the dying
with the stench of human decay.
It was a loud,
almost painful,
howling wind
that blew up over us
like the voices of all the dead.
It tore at his cloak ever more fiercely
until it finally blew it off.
And there Death stood,
not skeleton
nor partial being
more like some strange
crazed
stuffed creature,
unreal,
not alive
except for the eyes.
Unseeing or all seeing
they went on forever.
I screamed
then laughed.
Death was no more
than a doll.
This bizarre vision incensed me even more.

I was screaming,
"Fuck you death.
I have beaten you too many times.
You have nothing for me.
You are shit.
You are weak."
Screaming and raging
I grabbed death about the throat.
"You are nothing.
You are shit.
I will kill you."
I squeezed
with superhuman strength.
I started to strangle him
feeling the ultimate power of killing.
Taking a life,
not any life but death's life
or death.
I had power
not just over life and death of a man
but even over Death himself.
I was consumed with awesome strength.
Filled with passion
and blood lust
under the blood red moon.
I am strangling him
crushing his existence,
squeezing it through my fingers
and he's dying.
Squeezing more tightly,
I was killing death.
I was more powerful
than even he.
I was immortal.
I was invincible.
I was like a god
with power over life and death.
Not just humans
but over even Death itself.
I was more powerful than Death.
Squeezing more tightly

I noticed his eyes.
Not the eyes that I had seen before
but eyes that had seen everything,
seen everyone die before.
The people whose lives I had taken
multiplied by thousands,
tens of thousands,
millions.
And now there was a mouth,
a mouth that seemed to wear
a knowing smile
and with the eyes watching.
The eyes watching
smiling
like they enjoyed some private joke.
Like I had been tricked by the devil
and had given up my soul.
I was killing Death.
I was more powerful than death.
But in those eyes I saw
that I
was becoming Death.
Like some soul theft
or soul transference
I was going to be Death.
Slipping in
while he was slipping out.
I was killing Death
and to the victor goes the spoils,
Death.
I realized I was becoming Death
and forever would be witness to all the dying
everywhere, always.
I began to see with those eyes,
the deaths of newborn babies,
violently taken away and murdered.
Ravished,
beaten,
innocence defiled,
mothers screaming,
trying but dying.

Fathers, brothers,
daughters,
old people,
young people
violently losing the last breath.
Some going painfully,
some peacefully
but dying just the same.
Teased,
tormented,
beaten, eaten,
raped, pillaged,
filleted
and left for the elements to finish.
Septic,
necrotic,
insane,
born again, never born at all,
blessed, cursed,
disappeared,
remembered or not.
Dead,
dying,
life torn away.
The unfairness,
the capriciousness,
the viciousness,
the evil and accidents that end life.
All that.
Forever.
Always.
I'm becoming only Death.
I start to scream.
I'm not this bad.
I could never take this.
I try to cry out for all the dead,
my mouth open to the point of not having any jaws
like access to the underworld,
a megaphone for all below.
But there is no sound
except in my soul.

Cries, screams,
pain and regret.
The blood red moon
howled in my ears
and became the screams
that I could not hear
that passed over my lips.
Howling horror,
torment,
pain and suffering,
and never ending
death.

I leapt half of out of my bed
soaking wet,
hot like hell,
gasping for breath
and looking for Death.
I looked around.
There was no red moon.
There were no others.
I was alone.
Still alive
in flesh and body.
It wasn't me,
it couldn't be.
Although my heart was cold
it still beat.
I was human once more,
mortal
but saved.
Still,
I was marked by blood
and had to be careful.
Because deals were made,
sometimes in passion,
sometimes by mistake.
Deals extracted payment
beyond knowing
but due just the same.
Taking forever for my breathing to slow down,

or for my heart to stop beating through my chest,
or my eyes to focus
on a different reality in a different place,
until I can think ....was it real?
Or, do we have a deal?

THE ENEMY

Down
with leaders
who would so readily
send you to war.

They are the true enemy
of all mankind.

Not many men and women
want to rush forward
into their deaths
prematurely
with pain and agony.

You have to realize
there was no general
leading the troops at Gallipoli.

Foolish, scared men
rushing into death
stupid and victimized
and not for their own purpose.

Dashing into hard bullets
shrapnel
flying bodies
ripped and torn apart
for generals

far distant
much more concerned
with their own soft will
than the soft flesh
and organs
of people whose lives
they held in their hands.

Politicians
corrupt
bloated

evil men
who would for their own
devious purpose
manipulate
use and abuse
those within their power
for whatever
"good" reason
unto death
unto pain
agony
and destruction.

These are the true
anti-Christs in all times.

Even a benevolent dictator
is benevolent only to
some people
and in order for someone
to be rich and powerful
many, many more
have to suffer poverty
distress, disease
and play puppets
dangling on their strings.

When I came back from
my war
I had no doubt
who the enemy was.

Ho Chi Minh, General Giap
Lyndon Baines Johnson
Richard Nixon
and every conservative

liberal
son or daughter
who by ignorance
complacency
or conscious purpose
abused us.

I couldn't fault
those who didn't want to go
but I did hold in contempt
some of their reasons
for that decision.

I went in ignorance
into enlightenment
like too many
before me.

Half a million lost
in one battle in World War I.

The officer corps
the leadership
by birthright
and privilege

empowered dilettantes
deadly and merciless
about their business
playing war
playing life
with all our lives.

At Gallipoli
thousands of men
from thousands of miles away
casually discarded
for a losing cause.

the corrupt
horrific
moral only in the eyes
of the god
they worshipped
in the same casual
fashion.

My regret
coming back
a used dupe
was that there was no sympathy
for these people's destruction.

That their crimes
would go unpunished
even worse
unappreciated.

A man in Vietnam
a leader of men
leader at West Point
destined for great things
had a bad hair day
got scared
made a bad mistake
called a napalm air strike
on his own position
with the NVA
too far away
to feel that hot death.

He survived
unscathed

was immediately transferred
to a staff job
promoted
and given the distinguished service cross
the nation's second highest medal
for bravery.

Those few of his men that survived
told me he was a dead man
if they ever saw him again.

This hero
retired a three star general
well cared for
by his brethren.

Where is the justice
for people like him
for people
like all those
that with impunity
ruin
and torture
the lives of so many of us?

An argument
against karma
an argument
against justice

a painful reality
with us locked in
expendable
small time fries
and pawns
for the amusement
of a privileged few.

WHEN DEATH COMES

Whether it grabs you by the hair
sucks the air
out of your sails
whether you packed your bags
had better things to do
just fell in love
or wish you had

When death comes

Whether your prayers
are up to date
your bills are paid
you've read a good book
whether you're ready or not

When death comes

Whether it rips out your heart
whether you rail against it
fist clenched and impassioned
under the protection of heavenly bodies
or the cross
the atomic or hydrogen bombs
or enchantment

When death comes

Whether you pretend not to see it coming
not to hear the hard breathing
or smell the fetid breath
whether you brushed your teeth today
or ever
have dressed your best
or forgotten how

When death comes

Whether you want to
make a deal
be back in a minute
go to the bathroom
go around the corner
go home
go crazy
go away
go back to the beginning
go up
get down
sing a song
kiss lips
lick tips
suck various objects
make war
give love
whether you had something better in mind

When death comes

Whether you gave at work
whether you are
lost
looking
lonely
lazy
limp
lame
lovely
lucky
or just plain tired

When death comes

Whether you're
laughing
crying
smiling
hoping
dreaming
begging
or not quite ready

When death comes he's serious

Meet him at the door and say
"Oh, you want 1021 that's next door"
slam the door, run through the house
jump out the back window
and run for your life

You could meet him at the door
in disguise
say "hello"
run by him down the stairs
wait until he almost catches up
then turn around and trip him
shake him up

Or invite him in for a cup of tea
say "I know you're busy"
then fill his cup with too much life
he hates that
he will get you some time
but it would be bad form
to make it easy

You don't have to be polite
You don't have to be nice
Your only defense is life
So live it

UNINVITED MEMORIES

I am a haunted man
followed by visions
screaming spirits
and lost souls

A burden of my life
of my deeds
a price to pay for some experiences
some mistakes
or no reason at all

Not Casper the friendly ghost
not Marley wrapped in chains
and wailing
but the dead without judgment
in confused nonexistence
hovering
popping in and out of vision
screeching by with no direction

A price I pay all my days

I have no fear of these spirits
but I don't bear their company
comfortably
like a chill wind
or bad food
they unsettle me
cause me to pause and think

I have killed
creatures
birds and animals

I have killed other men
and strangely enough
never with personal malice

which makes no sense at all

I feel no shame
for their murder
but sad
uneasy and wondering

Why me
in their life what pacts
what deals have been made
that I became the agent
of such misery
horror
and death

Me
who loves life
and most people
believes in the Anglo-Saxon
need for kindness
now causing such pain

Did we meet in dreams
plan and scheme the play
wheel and deal
whose will forced on who

What vicious
sinister agreement transpired

I consciously sought out the experience
as a transformational exercise
in establishing my manhood
my right to personal power
in the world
with a price to pay

I pay it still
with this burden of souls
and spirits
and dues to pay

that cannot be written off for me
as karma
because I still find life too good
to take lightly

I did not kill for vengeance
to right a wrong
or do a right
I killed in the fight
for me to stay alive

Though I worked at it
performed the ritual
in the accepted ways
of my social structure
I struggled hard with the clash between
how it felt
and how it should look
how the dance was performed

I tried to make the steps right
to find the joy
the satisfaction
I was supposed to feel
and later even denied the shame
I was supposed to feel

Someone once casually asked
"What's it like to kill someone?"
I told them
that's too personal a thing

I'd much rather talk about
penis sizes
and who's more manly than who

HOW THE FUCK
DO YOU THINK IT FEELS
to bury a bush axe
in someone's skull
splitting flesh and bone

to spill out soft gray brain

To flex a finger
and see your power
rip apart muscle and flesh
that was another living
human being

You had to be there
is too weak a reply
you don't want to be there
is more honest

And you can't tell them
about the ghosts
that stain you
and threaten you
like collection agencies
for their due

It's not a memory
not an isolated act
it is an incredible responsibility

Unlike giving life
giving death
lasts forever
at least as long as memory

I walk my days on tightrope
trying to balance between
honoring these people
and keeping them out of my life

They would feed on it
because I took their own

I wish John Wayne or Rambo
faced that question
"What is it like to kill someone?"

Maybe some of us would have gone
traveling with more serious contemplation
of what we were in for

Maybe
I don't know what it's like to kill someone
but I do know what it's like for me
to kill someone

The spirit claims a toll
which is paid
dues are due

I remember a special forces sergeant
credited with the most confirmed
personal kills in Viet Nam
two hundred and sixty some
himself
within seven years dead of cancer

Something to think about
Mr. Rambo

If life becomes cheap
so is yours

I live with the hope
with the belief
that somehow
what I have done
is part of the plan

That there was some purpose
for the people
that paid the first blood
their wives and lovers' tears
children lost
mothers' and fathers' pain

If for some long term good

it is beyond me to see

I have killed
I am not ashamed of it
I am not proud of it
I tell myself I am not scared of it
and I will live with this

Live with each one of them
for a long
long
time

WELCOME BACK

The Chicago convention in 1968
my helmet
club
even Swiss army knife
taken away.

Sitting in
the back of a paddy wagon
jostling around
with a group of strangers
when someone
well dressed for the occasion
professional looking
and in their late twenties
turned to me and said,
"Is that your brother's jacket?"

Remarking about
the fatigue shirt that I wore
with combat infantryman's badge
airborne wings
patches and sergeant's stripes
on the sleeves
recondo patch on the chest.

Airborne
mobile guerrilla
I was shocked
and taken aback
and said, "What do you mean?"

He said,
"Is that
your older brother's shirt?"

I realized
he didn't think

I was old enough
to be in the army
and go to war.

The war
he was protesting against
with me.

I got pissed off
and yelled,
"What do you mean
my brother's shirt?
Who the fuck do you think
is fighting this war?

The average man killed
there is 19 years old.
Some of them
with pimples
still on their face
and virgin.

Usually snatched up
before they even have time
to think about it.

Maimed
killed
or deranged
before they are old enough
to get legally drunk
much less vote
for the people
that started the goddamn war.

No
this isn't
my older brother's shirt.
It's mine.
I've been there.

I've gone to the war.
I've been there in your place.
Jesus fucking Christ
don't you realize
Sergeant Rock
is only 19 or 20 years old?"

I was greeted by
hostile silence.
A nonverbal reprimand
for my bad taste
and politically unacceptable behavior.

I sat trembling with rage
and hurt
until we arrived
at the Cook County jail
where
I encountered the large
corn fed
simple minded
hostile
and mean
Chicago police
and realized
I had another fight tonight.

I took a slow breath
and got ready.

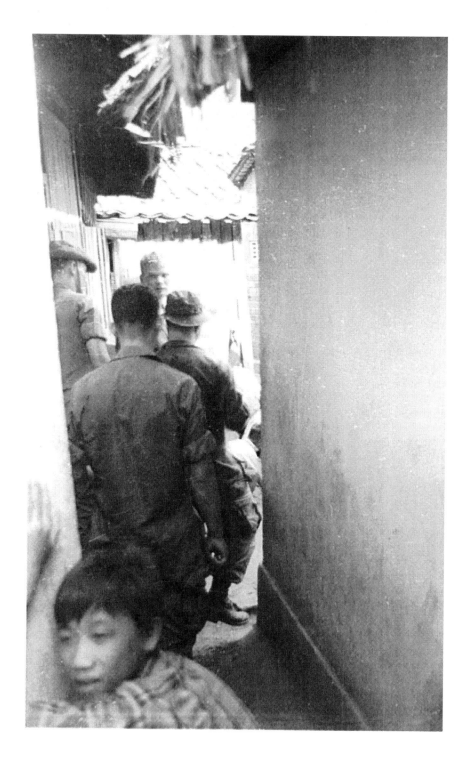

HERE'S TO US

Here's to the
walking wounded
the lame
drained
blamed
strugglers
trying to make it back
make sense
have sense
and believe

they came back
stained
framed
by the people
that sent them

scorned by those
whose place in history
they took

envied by a few
who wanted to go
but were relieved
they did not have to

here's to us
hated by damaged adversaries
used and abused
by our own politicians
lied to by our generals
lied to ourselves

toys for the brass boys
who lead us unto death
and despair
and even into

no longer caring

left by our lovers
wives
and even mothers

sold out
to the TV news

not even remembered
in the Viet Nam blues

lost
forgotten
not forgiven
ignored
left for bored
left without hope
or salvation

thanks for nothing
from a "grateful nation"

here's to the
walking wounded

we're still struggling
stumbling
not quite belonging

here's to us
thanks from us
because no one else
will give us
the satisfaction

WHY

let me make it real clear
I didn't go to Nam
to protect your rights
freedom for the American people
emancipation
of a suppressed peoples
freeing of the South Vietnamese
from the opposition
of communism
and tyranny

I went with one purpose
to face death
and in the process
mature
and become
a man

to pass the threshold
from adolescence
into male adulthood

cast off the shackles
of mothering
break through the bondage
of social propriety
and order

get down
get dirty
and come back
at the very least
romantically impaired

a more powerful being
a warrior
tested, fired

firmed up
by adversity
and the challenge
of eminent death
dirt
mud
and disease

it really never mattered
where it was
or who
we fought
or why we were going

just fire
and flame
to temper
our steel
make us stronger
wiser
and more capable
in the world

ha
what a surprise

I came back wiser
than I ever bargained for

ANOTHER SATURDAY NIGHT

Though the moon
was bright
shining in the night somewhere,
down on the earth floor
it was just light enough
to see shadows,
hints of movement.
The right mix
for hallucinating
or confusing realities.
The weather was somewhat cooler
than earlier in the day.
The sweat had dried up
making a tasty appetizer
for clouds of mosquitoes
out for dinner.
You sit leaning back
with your packs still on
in a close semi-circle
so you could reach out
and touch those on either side.
Each one pointing outwards
trying to see
in the near black
of triple canopy jungle.
Keeping the eyes moving
watching
for telltale signs
of hesitation
or quick movement.
Surrounded by a million
different noises
associated with nighttime
in the jungle.
Leaves rubbing
twigs falling
animals moving

through the shrubbery
on the ground
and through the trees.
Insects buzzing and screaming
sometimes so big
that you could hear them moving.
Altogether
it was a symphony of chaos.
A threat
noticed by sudden silence
surrounding movement
like an aura.
Smelling the air
trying to find scent
hidden among the musky earth smells
and too numerous plants and flowers.
Just able to see the trail edge
through an occasional leaf
or branch or tree.
Tired but wired.
Soon you'd be taking turns
trying to sleep
while the others keep watch.
All of you
trying to adjust
to the sudden change
to darkness.
Like turning off the lights
all the sounds and sights
of daytime transformed
and you're transported
into the night world.
Still hunting
still hunted
in the darkness.
Waiting
watching
and wondering
and more waiting.
Tired
but more comfortable

in a small piece of this world.
Fear
draining away with the fatigue.
A sudden quick movement
catches the eye
from across the trail.
The finger down immediately
to the selector switch
on the rifle.
Not quite ready
to wake anyone else.
Still the risk of embarrassment
outweighs the risk of death.
A darting movement
low and to the left.
Then you hear a shuffling sound
almost upon you
and just before you pull the trigger
you glimpse a large rodent snout
just as he notices your smell
quickly turns around
and scurries up the trail.
Flicking the selector switch
back to semi
taking a slow deep breath
and smile.
Glad you didn't wake anyone else up
to share this embarrassment.
Breath slowly moves through you
like a tranquilizer
you begin to settle down
and relax.
Start scanning
smelling
listening
and waiting.
Suddenly
you become aware of a quietness.
You're sure there is a quiet space
coming from the other side
and down the trail

that's real.
Something's out there.
The insects are quiet
and hiding.
Something is out there.
You don't know how long it's been.
It's always so hard
to recognize the start of silence.
Shit
were you drifting
not paying attention?
Damn
something is out there.
You slowly reach over
squeeze the arm of the man
on your left.
You feel him squeeze back.
He's awake.
Squeeze the man on the right
and he responds.
He's awake.
You turn your head to each
point to your ear
then down the trail to your right
and shake your fingers quickly
about your ear.
Their heads raise up off their packs
and turn in that direction.
Their hands move over
to their selector switches
as they squeeze the other members
on their sides.
Listening
the silence remains.
The shadows are dancing
flipping across the trail.
Is there something really out there?
Maybe it's just a large animal.
Still listening,
then you hear a clink
metal

clinking against metal.
No wild rodent carries canteens.
Somebody else
is coming down the trail
Charlie.
You hear some shuffling
maybe some soft voices.
You quickly look around.
Everybody's up
attentive
still lying on their backs.
Weapons are brought around
more in the right direction.
The claymore handle
is made more available.
The wire safety pulled back down.
Slow breaths
don't touch the adrenaline
shooting through your veins.
Everyone is keyed up.
How many are there?
Will they see you?
Eyes are bright
faces painted with military crayon
mosquitoes' buzzing
forgotten.
Smells and subtle hints
no longer noticed.
More shuffling
more tones and speaking.
Then you see the first one
walking on the right side of the trail.
No black pajamas
olive drab uniform
glimpsed portions of an AK-47 followed by a man
with a grenade launcher
talking softly
but too loud for the jungle.
They are too relaxed
too comfortable.
That means there must be

too many.
The Ho Chi Min sandal
strikes the ground
inches from your foot.
You can see the toes
even in the dark
you wonder how dirty the nails are.
They are so close
you can smell them
the wood smoke
the stale sweat and dirt.
The breathing becomes shallow
trying not to exist for anyone else.
No movements
except for the slow directing of rifles.
You're as scared
as you can possibly be
without screaming.
The hand gripping the claymore handle
waiting for the hint
of any hostile acknowledgement.
You wish you could see
more down the trail.
At the same time
wish you could just close your eyes
and disappear.
You turn to look at the others
and see what seem to be
large white eyes
staring out of the dark.
You try to will them
into squinting
to hide these beacons
in the bushes.
This is the part you hate
the waiting
for death.
Not knowing
what shit will come down.
Not knowing
what you're up against.

Not acting
just waiting
fearing
not moving
and barely breathing.
More people walk by.
It seems they are more relaxed
the further down they come.
Rifles slung around their shoulders
not ready
still talking
comfortable.
This is their neighborhood.
Not expecting any muggings.
More clinking canteens or rifle belts
not taped for silence.
You're counting.
Trying to recognize any patches
or insignias
recognize weapons
distracting yourself
from too many
armed and unfriendly people
walking right by your feet.
Suddenly
someone trips before you
making noise
and maybe cursing in Vietnamese.
Then there is a hesitation.
You can see part of the chin
and mouth
and one eye
looking down at the ground.
Looking down at the ground
where the claymore was
and may have not been
well enough disguised.
His head snaps up
looking startled in your direction
and your hand
squeezes the claymore handle.

The world erupts in a loud explosion
dust, leaves,
branches, twigs
and people flying.
Screams
all your rifles firing.
Jumping up at the same time
packs slumping down on the back
releasing spent ammo magazines
quickly replacing them
firing more.
You yell "180.... 100
Now!"
and your group begins a wild dash
into the bushes.
Firing in order
and running from the trail.
Screaming and returning fire
the slower rate of an AK-47 picking up
and joining into a loud roar.
Most of those in front of you
on the trail
are down
moaning or still.
You glimpse as you turn
and see so many green uniforms
rifles moving up
sprouting bright muzzle flashes.
You fall back
one firing then turning to run
then the next one
picking up the firing.
No longer waiting
no longer wondering
no longer thinking
just running.
Smashing through the brush
on automatic.
The dice are thrown
and you're just along for the ride.
Crashing through the jungle

bullets still cracking about you
tearing up trees and earth.
Explosions falling behind you
dirt, shrapnel and foliage
join the bullets.
They seem to think
you're more behind the trail.
You're no longer shooting
just running
scared to death
but so alive
and wanting to stay that way.
Still crashing through the bush.
The rifle fire and explosions
that seemed so deafening before
are fading
and seeming to be directed
somewhere you're not.
Gasping in deep breaths
searching in the darkness and trees
trying to find everybody.
Not daring to even whisper
you snap your fingers
and wait for replies.
First one then another
then a third.
Someone's not here.
You move close
kneeling down in the bush.
You put your heads together
everyone barely able
to catch their breath.
You notice who is missing
"Did anyone see him go down?"
Gasping heads shake no.
"Well, at least they don't know
where we are."
Suddenly
more shouting in Vietnamese
more rifle fire with bright flashes
bullets breaking up the world

about you.
One of you says "Shit"
and nobody cares who did
"270.......150"
you almost shout in a whisper.
You're up and running
somehow moving like magic
through the thick growth.
Bullets and debris
hammering into the ground.
Bullets slapping and breaking trees.
A loud explosion off to the left
knocks you down
and rolls you over onto your side.
Ears ringing
sounds muffled
back up and running
gasping
not shooting
trying to disappear.
Stumbling
running
until you can barely breathe at all.
Sucking the air in
like hot flames
you can't catch you breath.
So you pull up
and fall to a knee.
Not hearing very well
trying to see.
Snapping your fingers
to no reply.
Snap again
still no answer.
Everything's moving
but not hearing
bullets crashing here.
They've moved off to the right.
The air is full of the acrid
pungent smell of gun smoke.
You can still hear people

shouting in Vietnamese
but further down
and still to the right.
Snap your fingers again
and listen.
First one
then another reply.
You wonder who else is missing
then you hear a third snap.
Together
moving slowly through the trees
breathing so hard now
you can't understand
why they don't hear you
but just in case you try to be quiet.
You're together
only four
one long gone.
Down on one knee again
with heads together
blasting each others faces
with deep ragged breaths
you pull out the compass
and try to remember
how far you've gone
and in what direction
from the ambush site.
Then try to figure the nearest place
for a chopper pick-up.
It will take you hours to get there
if you're lucky.
Hours
with too many NVA looking
and it's night.
You're pretty sure which way it is
show everybody the compass
and after slow
finger walking movements
point the direction,
lean over to one man
and tell him

he's replacing the missing one.
You open your eyes wide
and look at everybody.
They nod their heads.
"Let's get the fuck out of here,"
they seem to say.
You look at the point man
and whisper,
"Let's go."
You move out
exhausted legs like lead
and begin your slow ballet
through the jungle.
Trying not to make any sound
almost too tired to move at all.
The adrenaline somewhat burned off.
Fatigue,
not enough to chase away
the flight rush
and fear,
starts creeping back in.
Trying to keep it in check
but relishing the effect
as it
tunes up the hearing
sensitizes the nostrils
and brings new levels of hallucination to the vision.
You slowly dance your way
through the trees
hoping
wondering
and waiting.
Still too caught up in the fear
and post rush letdown
to wonder
if any of you will get out of here
alive
and a song drifts across
your tired brain.
"It's another Saturday night
and I ain't got nobody.

Got some money
cause I just got paid...."
You smile
until you realize with a shock
just where you are.
Ballet movements
slow though the trees and bushes
smelling the earth again
musky ripe.
Feeling leaves brush against your side
eyes looking around
hoping and not hoping
to see anything.
Rechecking the compass
hoping this is the right direction.
Hoping no one hears you.
Hoping this is not your turn
to die.

CAMPFIRE TALES

I was new in country.
I had been there only about a month.
Long enough to prove I wasn't chicken
and handled myself in combat.
We were sitting around a fire one night
in the highlands of Dak To on the Cambodian border.
I don't remember this guy's name
but he was short, soon to go home, within weeks.
He had been from Detroit or New Jersey
or somewhere like that,
time has dimmed the exact place.
His wife was a beautiful woman
who had caught the eye
of some fairly ranking mob guy.
She had been flattered, interested
and things became more serious.
It came to the point
where this man could leave town
or be killed,
one or the other.
A gentleman's opportunity was being offered.
This guy could leave town
and stay alive
while this mob guy played around with his wife.
Maybe at some point the guy
would get tired of her
and the man could come home.
So,
he went into the Army,
did his training, paid his dues
and ended up in a Long Range Reconnaissance Patrol unit
in the highlands of Vietnam.
He changed.
With time and combat
he had changed.
As we sat around the fire,
he told me how much he had changed.

99

He was talkative which was unusual for him.
After two years,
he was going to face what he left behind.
An unfaithful wife
and some mob guy
who had threatened his life with earnest intent
had changed him.
Being in combat repeatedly
had changed him.
Killing and chasing death
had changed him.
Facing death often enough
had changed him.
Wading through crotch deep mud
swarmed by leeches
and masses of mosquitoes sucking his precious fluids
had changed him.
Dancing around bullets,
exploding earth
and flying metal
had changed him.
Having no hope of any other life
or any life at all
had changed him.
He had nothing,
nothing left to lose.
With time,
death and destruction took it's toll.
Took away conscience and compassion
in exchange for death,
destruction and hopelessness.
The custom was to take a trophy
from the dead
in the form of an ear,
cut off and placed in a salt filled pouch
carried on our belts.
This became our unit's insignia
since we weren't allowed one on our uniforms
or allowed to carry any other form of identification.
Just tiger-striped camouflage fatigues
and strange weapons.

He had changed enough.
He was empowered enough.
He decided to confront his past
as a new man.
He sent to his wife and the mobster
a little package for each.
A small package
with minimal wrapping of brown paper,
tied with string
and just a brief card inside.
The signed card said,
"Looking forward to seeing you soon."
Of course, in each package with the card
was a mummified ear.
At this point in the story
you could see that he was enjoying himself
and he would smile
then be quiet for a while.
After a few moments
he would finish his tale.
So, in like two weeks
he gets a letter from his wife,
which was very fast in those days
because it usually took longer
to get letters from the States.
The letter had professed her love
and sorrow
that things had not gone right,
her commitment to working it out
and how much she truly
cared for him.
Now,
he had a really good time with this
and would even laugh a little.
But the story wasn't over.
Maybe a week after that
he got another letter,
this one from the mobster,
professing his respect
and appreciation for him.
Swearing there was a grievous misunderstanding,

101

that he had no evil designs on him
and was sorry about any grief
past events had caused him.
Whatever the guy and his wife had
it had been a brief,
ill-conceived affair
and he regretted it greatly.
He was sure the soldier could understand
man to man
that this was a minor glitch in life
and could be readily put behind,
hinted that he respected him
for going the way he did,
serving his country
and suggesting some future employment was possible.
It apparently ended on a friendly,
brotherly note.
Well,
this guy would laugh a soft chuckle.
He would really, really enjoy this
because he was free,
by reason of war insanity,
of the usual constraints,
fears, and inhibitions
that ruled the regular stateside life.
If he had a weapon
he could kill without remorse.
Even without a weapon
he could be very deadly
if motivated with desire.
This was so liberating,
so empowering he was born again
as a new man,
maybe a demon
but a powerful entity in his own right.
He could walk tall and fearless
in the streets
where he walked as prey before.
He could stand up to even the mob
because he didn't play by any rules.
He could be more ruthless

and at the same time passionate.
It was not just business
it was personal.
I couldn't help but share his pleasure.
I couldn't help but be encouraged
by the possibility
that out of all this killing and craziness
someone could be positively transformed.
The supreme confidence,
erectile function,
James Bond was just a repressed queer,
Scar Face just an impotent businessman.
No one has more power
or causes more fear on any playing field
than the berserker.
It gave me hope.
It gave me ambitions.
I couldn't help but smile myself.

CAMPFIRE TALES PART TWO

Another guy I met
when I first joined the unit
was a short timer
they called the Ranger,
a least, that's the only name I ever heard used.
In days when not many people went to Ranger school,
he had gone.
He was a staff sergeant with little time left.
These were the days when this unit
had been fighting the Vietcong for a couple of years.
These men were professional,
used to winning and confident.
These men were going home
before they met the North Vietnamese army
every day
and things changed.
The Ranger had changed, as well,
during his time in Vietnam.
He was a lifer,
a career guy.
He planned on spending his 20 in the army.
He did not expect to become an officer
or become a general,
just be a sergeant,
make good money
and do his time.
But he had changed.
The killing,
the maiming,
losing friends
and more killing
had changed him.
His ritual was similar for all the new guys.
There were new replacements regularly
depending on how many people had been killed,
wounded or rotated out.
This was a very small unit,

platoon size.
When I first ran into him it was before a campfire
in the highlands of Vietnam.
Then we would sit around a fire at night
between missions,
bullshit and carry-on.
The newer people would lie
about all cool things they had done.
The old-timers would lie
about some of the things they had done.
About what we had to look forward to
they were pleasantly honest
and horrifying.
You could tell they enjoyed it
but didn't feel it the same way
as the new guys did.
They lived it for so long
they believed it
and became sometimes hard, sometimes numb,
sometimes apathetic,
sometimes just scared and crazy.

It was considered by all
bad form
to lose it
and admit the weakness of fear.
Even when you talked of fear
you talked bravely.
Even when you felt apprehension
you remained aloof
and beyond it.
Even when you admitted shitting in your pants
you laughed about it.
Even when your friend
was shot to shit
you talked about it in a detached,
humorous or at least indifferent way.
The sole Truth was
that the only sin
was admitting that you were afraid.
You could murder

with enthusiasm and brutality.
You could ravage and maim
without conscience.
You could be selfish
and evil.
You could be filthy, ugly,
disgusting and rude.
You could be drunk, stoned,
hateful, vengeful,
Christian, romantic,
poetic, gay,
short, tall,
fast or slow.
You could be a cow fucker, bird lover,
intellectual, moron,
a priest or blasphemer.
You could be just about anything
but afraid.
This was unacceptable,
to be undeniably,
unashamedly,
uncontrollably
afraid
because almost everyone really was,
at least
some of the time.

I got nervous before a fight,
before the shooting had begun
when you knew
it was about to happen.
When you were surrounded,
when the enemy was close enough to spit on,
when you knew
it was just a matter of time.
The anticipation of the pain,
of the discomfort of mortal wounds
or torture
slid quickly around my brain in record speed
with horrifying impact and detail.
It would unsettle me,

cause me discomfort
and make me anxious for the fight to start,
to get it over with.
For once the first shot was fired,
the first explosion rang out
through the bush,
the first scream
or cry of injury
or violence,
I was in some other world.
My body did what it did
and I was along for the ride.
No fear,
no joy,
just a clear head
supercharged physical motivation
dwelling in a timeless space.
Maybe,
after running for hours
or sustained combat intermittently over days
the hormones would burn off,
I would become fatigued,
become somewhat apathetic,
or at least less enthusiastic.

For the Ranger
his usual routine was to talk calmly
to the new guys.
Be friendly and supportive
and when they began to feel comfortable
he would,
during the ongoing,
casual conversation,
slowly take something
out of the pouch on his belt.
In a slow,
determined way
that would obviously draw everyone's attention.
Then
he would take out his bowie knife,
which we all carried on our web gear

and maintained razor sharp.
Next
he would take this shriveled up ear
that he had pulled out of his pouch,
stab it
with the tip of the knife
continuing an undistracted conversation,
place it over the fire,
slowly roasting the mummified ear.
After a short time cooking
he would casually inspect the ear
and bring it to his mouth,
bite off a piece
and chew it.
All this,
delivered in a casual,
matter-of-fact style
not skipping a beat in the conversation.
It was some judge of your character
that you tolerated this,
or a least did not throw up
or otherwise embarrass yourself.
If you did,
that was pretty much it.
It was like a rite of passage.
If you could not tolerate a little cannibalism
you might not have what it takes.

By the time I became
one of the old guys
things had changed.
The action had picked up.
When you killed soldiers
you barely had time to collect information
and booby trap a body.
Usually you had no time at all
except to run.
We were always outnumbered
sometimes
by only ten to one,
sometimes

by a hundred to one
but always,
outnumbered.
The enemy was well armed,
well trained
and disciplined.
We were lucky
if we got away with our lives
much less trophies.

I didn't meet anybody else
like these two guys again,
and fortunately
didn't have to be just like them either.
I did become empowered
in some ways,
confident I could kill people,
was good at it
and apparently able to do it
without too much obvious angst
or anger.
I felt some discomfort
and unease
with the whole process.
I couldn't help but care
that I may have been used.
I couldn't get comfortable
with the empathy I felt
for the people I was fighting.
That made me some kind of criminal,
not Robin Hood
but a hooded Robin.
Not a freedom fighter
but a dupe
or insignificant pawn.
All in all
it was a losing proposition.
If I didn't fight well
I'd die.
If I killed at all
my soul was damned.

All in all,
a bad deal.
I missed the good old days
I never had.

BROTHERS

Where are my brothers?
Where are the memories
of my brothers?

Not brothers by blood
or even preference
but brothers in blood
by necessity.

Brothers in sickness
till death do us part
though hardly ever
in health
wealth
or happiness.

Where are my brothers?
Where did they go?
What became of such innocent
abused youth?

Yes, I know
some of us became lame
lame in limb
lame in life
and in brain.

Others lost
in the fatal sense of present
physical reality.

Where are they?
What became of them?
Their names
on a large black slice of rock
buried in the nation's capital
appropriate

but not satisfactory.

Remembered on a popular TV show
where models of beauty
they never saw
gestalt, moan and
bewail the horrors
of their passing
smacking of blasphemy
at the same time
sexually titillating.

Where are my brothers?
I'm not seeking sisters.
Where are my brothers?

The brothers I didn't like
brothers I hated
brothers I despised
brothers we were
till death do us part.

The bloodlines external
real blood brothers
real pus brothers
real brothers in the shit.

Brothers lying to each other
beating our chests
puffing
strutting
panting and
pretending.

Anything
for strength
and encouragement
for those few
who really believed it.

Brothers in the mud

mixed with the blood
leeches
so fat and juicy
they could leave you
wet dreams after falling off
from theirs.

Brothers wet and muddy
for so long
our skin became
permanently shriveled.

Brothers in the death dance
rolling
tumbling
screaming for joy
in bloodlust
and murder
no matter how brief.

Where are my brothers?
Walking disguised
as Clark Kent
stumbling, embarrassed
and in hiding
or strutting proud
and neurotic.

What happened with us?
What happened to us?
What happened in spite of us?
We did not live the only war.

Are we all brothers?
The family resemblance
seems so distant.
Who are my brothers?

Can brothers speak
different languages

like a family divided?

Can brothers kill
each other?

Where are my brothers?
Some gone too soon
to bones and rot.
Some so festered
and rotten
even I was unable to claim them.

Some just in the deep sleep
calm but departed.
Some falling down in pain
and anger
screaming
defiant
but still, nonetheless
very dead.

Some just slipped away
and quietly disappeared.

Some
becoming one with the universe
as one thousand, nine hundred and eighteen
pieces of flesh and bone
instant communication
and fertilization
no remnant even
for mom and dad.

Where are my brothers?
Will someone
someday
in the distant future
unearth
the collapsing bones
and say,
"Here they are"?

But they're not.
That's just their bones.

I used to think
life so suddenly gone
proved we were nothing more
than blood, bones and meat.

Now, I think there is more.
But what is it?
Where is it
and does it remember me?

Is there life only
while I remember them?

There are some brothers
now hiding behind
rolls of adult,
no longer baby,
fat.

There are some brothers
hiding behind tears
smiles
and now false teeth.

How can we be brothers
for such a short time?
How can we be so intensely related
and then so totally forgotten?

Were we so intimate
too intimate
too vulnerable
to the horror?

Confronting our deaths
together
naked

all pretenses dropped
like your pants
in the quick test
movement of the bowels
so familiar to the occasion.

Are we now afraid
to face each other?
To face ourselves
shamed and fearful
of the kinds of gods we were,
of the abuses of our power,
of the thrill we felt?

Hiding the evil
from people who think we are nice
reasonable
and just like them.

Where are my brothers?
Where are those just like me?

We are
fucked over
fucked with
fucked around.
I hope we are not all
still
fucked up.

Where are my brothers?

STEPS

It's as personal as sex.
Giving life and taking life
are such private,
usually hidden
occupations.
Both can be horrendous experiences,
for those that do
and those that watch.
In dealing death,
how you live it,
how you live with it
can be incredibly different
from one person to the next.
Sometime in private,
sometime in public,
sometime only in your dreams,
but to take real living meat
and make just plain meat
should move your very soul.
Making love has a depth of intimacy
that can be as profound as anything.
Bonding between two physical bodies
in such an open and personal way
can be a transcendental experience.
So can killing another person.
However,
instead of seeing God
you will probably see the devil.
Instead of gently touching
another's soul passionately,
you will be destroying one.
Private,
individual,
intimate manifestation
of a human capacity for good and bad,
love or hate,
giving or taking.

You can kill
with no passion
just like you can kiss
lifelessly.
You can love
like there is no tomorrow
and you can die
like there is no today.
How you are the next day
or afterwards,
how your conscience filters through you
are just as individual
and unique.
Are you a cold,
one-night-stand lover?
Are you so hollow
that even bringing death
and destruction
leaves you unmoved?
Are you more afraid of loneliness
or life itself?
Are you willing and able
to give and receive
or just into taking?
How much more personal can you be
with anyone
than to be inside them
and take their soul
along with internal organs
and life's blood?
You can find yourself in cosmic love
or lose yourself totally
in the horror of what you have done.
Like loving,
killing is a very personal thing.
What you give
you can't take back.
Once you've offered up
to the gods of life and revelry
or demons of the darkness,
you don't get to take it back.

Every man and woman
builds their own place
for pleasure or suffering.
How you touch the world
is how it touches you back.
How you give
is what you receive.
One small step for man
can mean anything for all mankind.
How you move through life
defines who you are.
At least as much
as who you are determines
how you live.
For every person
there is another possibility
and for every two people
there are 200 possibilities.
How hard it is for any language
to bridge so many different realities.
Each step we take
leaves a mark on the earth
for some time.
When the mark is worn away
do we no longer exist?
Are we no longer remembered
by the earth?
Each breath you take
is that much more of a commitment
to your reality.
Each step you take
is another effort
to be part of this world
in your body.
Who can know
the last step you will be held responsible for?
What last step
will truly mark your path
and passing?

LIES

I've heard too much
Too many excuses
Too many reasons
it had to be that way

The inevitable hardships
of war

Not enough time to prepare
No time for planning
for equipping
for understanding the people
the terrain

Somehow the radios aren't compatible
The back up and support can't reach that far
Events couldn't be foreseen
The intelligence was wrong
wasn't available
didn't reach us in time
There is no one else to do the job
You're all we have
The mission is more important
than your lives

On and on the excuses roll out
so you go out
under-prepared
under-equipped
blind

A sacrifice
for the cause
for the victory
you won't get to share
for real estate only important today
for something so valuable

your life
becomes a cheap price

But no general will pay
No politician will be discomforted
The contract suppliers
will never know
the smells
the pain

When it all falls apart
and bodies are tested and torn
their wives, lovers
friends and children
won't be left crying
won't be touched
by the dying

I don't believe the excuses
the burden
soldiers are asked
to rise above

These are lies
told by politicians
incompetent, immoral
or just indifferent

Told by generals
who grew out of soldiers
like some fungal forest growth
into politicians

The lying
the dying
goes on
as long as there is someone
who believes

FIRE SUPPORT BASE BLUES

There was some worry
about the increased activity of the North Vietnamese army
in the mountains on the western front.
This was thick terrain
and there were few natural landing areas available.
It was decided that we would infiltrate
through a fire support base
located as far from the main body of troops
and as close to the mountains as possible.
This was unusual enough
that it made us nervous.
After all,
if we could not find a place for the helicopter to drop us off
how were we going to find a place
for the helicopter to land and pick us up?
This usually meant that they would extract us
on the ends of ropes tied to sand filled ammo cans
thrown down through the jungle canopy.
This form of extraction was invariably fatal
to some at least.
Out of a team of five
bad odds.
This was supposed to be
an emergency form of extraction only.
Here we were being asked
to take it as routine.
The need to know
overruled the need to live
for some of us.
We landed in the middle of a small fire support base
in the middle of nowhere
surrounded by thick, triple canopy jungle.
There was just enough room
for a helicopter to set down in the middle
without hitting any of the bunkers
or canons arranged around the circular perimeter.
It reminded me of the Old West

when you would circle the wagons
and hold out for salvation
in the form of charging cavalry
with horns blaring.
As we had flown in
we all noticed how dense the jungle had been
all the way there.
No openings, clearings
or even obvious rivers that may have wide banks.
Nothing around
and it looked like nobody was home
but we knew better.
This fire support base had been getting attacked regularly
and taking moderate casualties.
The major who had been commanding this artillery outpost
was waiting on a stretcher
to be medevaced out on the chopper we flew in on.
As they lifted him up on the stretcher
to replace us on the helicopter
the men around the fire support base began cheering,
clapping and yelling.
The major appeared touched and emotional
as he waved back.
I couldn't tell if the men were glad
and expressing relief he was leaving
or, in fact,
if they were appreciating something about him as a commander.
It was hard to tell in this war.
The little existing bunker space
was not available to us.
We were used to living out in the open
so we just went and laid against the berne
which consisted of some sandbags
interspersed between occasional armored personnel carriers
and 105 howitzers
pointing out into the jungle.
The other troops were nervous around us.
We were like an alien race in some ways,
in tiger striped camouflage fatigues,
seriously armed
and pumping up for combat.

They got to fight standing up
with their buddies
and large cannons all around.
There was an armored personnel carrier facing out
about every third howitzer.
Everything was facing the thick, dark jungle.
Beyond the berne
there was a brief cleared area of maybe 50 yards
that looked like someone had taken a crude lawn mower
to chop down all vegetation
and stopped suddenly at a wall of jungle.
In fact,
they had just shot down the vegetation that was close by.
We were late enough that we had missed chow.
The artillery did not want to share anyway
as all the supplies had to be flown in daily
which was somewhat of a problem
because they were taking incoming fire regularly
and they knew they were surrounded
by good size unit of North Vietnamese army regulars.
This seemed to be another one
of the illogical military manifestations.
Everybody knew where the enemy was,
they were around all these guys.
Yet,
we were expected to go through all this effort
to find the very same enemy.
Just because they were hiding
underground or behind trees
didn't mean that you couldn't figure out
where they were.
These artillerymen were stationed
way out here
so that they could give artillery support
for units far way from the main body.
They had large units getting ambushed regularly
and always calling for fire support.
There really wasn't much room anywhere to sack out.
We set up next to one of the howitzers
where there was a bit of extra space
a few yards from the canon itself.

The artillerymen stared at us
with apprehension
as if we could bring some misfortune
with all our sneaking around in the jungle.
These guys
had been getting clobbered for weeks.
Towards us, their emotions
seemed to range from fear
to apprehension.
It seemed scary enough to them
just to sit around where they were,
loaded for bear
with many cannons and armored personnel carriers.
They had all kinds of things
to shoot at the enemy.
Yet, here we were
with just the packs on our back
and what ammo we could carry on our web gear,
ready to go sneaking out into that jungle
where,
every night they were reminded,
lots of NVA lived.
These were the moments I really disliked.
The sitting around,
waiting to be waiting
to do something.
The artillery men were mostly naked
from the waist up
and covered in a fine red dust.
It was hot and very dusty
where the jungle had been blown away
for this little outpost.
I was passing the time braiding some grass
in some sort of near meditative trance
when one of the guys came over
and offered me a smoke.
I told him no thanks
because it would be too easy to smell in the jungle.
We talked for a while about what had been going on
in their little part of the world.
He told me that the major who had been wounded

was actually a good guy.
He was always cussing out the people in the rear
when they were too slow to help out
his beleaguered, little outpost and men.
Now, all that was left
were a handful of sergeants
and a first lieutenant who was in command.
The helicopters had been sporadic
in supplying them over the last week
because there was a big push
on the other side of the valley
that had been taking up all their resources.
The rumored plan was to push the enemy in their direction
where they could be boxed in
and annihilated.
Somebody
had been reading textbooks again.
The artilleryman said it wasn't too bad
because they never ran out of ammo
and once in while
the NVA got so close
they could load their cannons
with what amounted to huge shotgun shells
and fire point-blank into the masses of troops.
He laughed a little nervously
as he described this to me.
I think he was trying to impress me,
this sneaky, guerrilla guy,
already growing a few days of facial hair
with how brave they were.
Jesus, I thought
they were crazy to sit out in the middle of the jungle
daring people to overrun them.
This was nuts.
I'd go hide out
and dance around the jungle any day.
His buddies were looking over enough
to make him feel uncomfortable
because he kept looking back in their direction
as if trying to figure out if it was all right.
He asked me what we were going to do.

I told him at first light
there was going to be a diversion on the other side of the compound
while we would sneak into the jungle
and go find some NVA.
He said, " That's stupid.
They're right out there."
"Yeah," I said.
"But we can sneak behind them
and call in some really bad shit.
It's cool to be better at this shit than Charlie is."
He looked at me strangely.
This guy asked me,
"What is that thing?"
pointing to the sword handle of the bush axe
taped upside-down on the left side of my web gear.
I unsnapped it
and pulled it out to show him what it was.
"See, this has a blunt tip for smashing into things,
a sharp, long blade for chopping up things
and it has this nice little a hook
which is perfect for taking ears."
This took him by surprise.
"No shit."
" Yeah."
Then I showed him my little pouch filled with salt
for carrying ears after they were taken.
"Do you have any on you?" he asked.
" No," I replied. "Why would I be taking ears out with me?
I'm going out to get some."
"Well, what do you do with them?" he asked.
"Freak people out
and prove to the intelligence fucks that what we say is true.
Dragging around whole bodies is too much of a hassle."
"You guys are crazy," he said.
After a short interval,
he moved back over with his buddies
occasionally looking back over at us
and shaking his head.
What can I say?
I was a 20 year-old guy
trying to find some sort of validation

for the insanity I lived in,
to get some kind of appreciation
for what I was doing,
even if it was fear and loathing.
It was just a slight variation on bicycle tricks.
Otherwise,
I'd be knee deep in reality.
By this time we had started to paint up
so that we could get out early in the morning
before it was truly light.
Somehow this unnerved the people watching.
I could dig it.
Put on a little show
to terrorize these young guys
who got to sleep back here every night.
They didn't know what it was like
to be running through the jungle
chewed up,
shot up
and hounded by lots of well-armed, pissed off people.
It was easy to cop an attitude
in this war.
An attitude that everybody else
had it better than we did.
It was sometimes true
but plenty of other guys got killed
in all kinds of ways.
It became dark.
We were bored and had nothing better to do
so we started to sack out at the base of the howitzers.
We just lay down on our back backs on the ground,
tilted our hats over our eyes
and tried to get some sleep.
It wasn't too long
before a fire mission was called
and the canons started going off.
The first few rounds got us up
and paying attention,
trying to figure out if shit was coming down on us
or somewhere else.
Each time the cannon fired

it literally lifted us up off the ground a couple of inches.
But we were cool and the elite.
We couldn't complain about it.
I figured that if they got into some kind of rhythm
it would be like riding on a bouncing train
and I could get some sleep.
I tried.
It was really hard
until the sound made me so deaf
I couldn't hear well anymore.
I got used to being raised up off the ground
and flopping back down every few minutes or so.
At some point
I actually did fall asleep
because the next thing I knew
someone was shaking me awake
to get ready to go.
This didn't take much
because my pack was my pillow
and my rifle was in my hand
and breakfast was a fig bar
of some unknown denomination.
I got up and took a piss
where I had been sleeping
about the same time green tracers started passing overhead
from the other side of the compound.
There was all kinds of shouting going on
and soon there was returning fire
from 50 caliber machine guns on the APCs
and an occasional howitzer firing beehive rounds into the jungle.
It was still dark
and the flashes looked orange and dirty.
We decided this was as good time as any
and made our way between sandbags
and one of the howitzers.
We moved quickly into the tree line 50 yards away.
Once we made our way into the dark canopy
we set up a perimeter and listened for a while.
After we had not heard anybody moving about nearby
we slowly got up
and ballet danced our way through the jungle.

We had moved only a hundred yards
when we started to take rounds,
friendly rounds
judging by the color of the tracers.
Some overzealous,
paranoid,
trigger happy Americans
apparently had forgotten
or had not been told we just had gone out.
We just hunkered down as low as we could
and waited for about 10 minutes
until it all chilled out.
Then we got up,
bent over more than usual
and moved more quickly than usual
away from these guys.
Not surprisingly,
we found the North Vietnamese army
everywhere.
Our job was not to fight
this time,
but to count them
and radio back where they were headed.
We were out for three or four days
and were lucky enough towards the end
to locate a small clearing
which had been a Montagnard homestead at one time.
This allowed us to be extricated
without being dragged through the trees.
On the helicopter ride back
I was talking to one of the door gunners
who told me that the fire support base
had been hit by a battalion size unit
two days after we left.
They had been firing beehive rounds
and after that, regular rounds
all night long.
They ran out of ammunition
before dawn and any helicopter support could come in.
The NVA were shooting up the armored personnel carriers
with incendiary rounds

that burned up anybody who had the bad judgment
to seek shelter in them.
The gunner said he was on the second or third run in that morning
and there were bodies
everywhere.
The Vietnamese and Americans all mixed up
in a tangled mess.
He said the survivors
were all dirty,
bloody and so tired
they didn't seem to care about anything anymore.
After all the bodies were picked
up an infantry unit was brought in
to search through the jungle
for remaining North Vietnamese.
Of course,
all they found were the weapons
and bodies left behind
with the occasional booby trap
to keep things interesting.
Huge helicopters flew in
to remove the damaged and broken equipment
and brought in new replacements.
They kept the fire support base for another week and a half
until it was decided
that it was no longer necessary
and everything was packed up
and pulled out.
They counted over a hundred NVA dead
making this a real "victory".
However,
there were many American dead
and many more wounded.
Headquarters always lied about American casualties
but there were, for sure,
piles of dead.
All these men dying
or losing chunks out of their souls
for a small, dirty little patch
in the middle of a thick,
unfriendly jungle

not near any thing or anybody else.
Another glorious victory
for democracy and the USA.
Letters were written,
officers promoted,
medals given
and bodies
some breathing,
some not,
finally went home.
Where
"white lightning was still
the biggest thrill of all",
clouds of hair spray
lacquered hair into some order
and the day's Vietnam body count
was politely declared
on the Evening News.

CALLOUS HEART

Slowly,
insidiously like a creeping vine
over the jungle floor,
you don't see it coming.
You don't feel it until you become surprised,
seemingly suddenly
by its presence and reality.

The whole idea of violence
and killing
is both exciting and terrifying
initially.

When faced with the reality
whether it's brutal,
a fair fight,
or you lose,
friends,
body parts
or your courage,
it becomes so much more
predominantly terrifying.

It becomes gradually
more difficult to maintain
a high state of terror.
If you can survive,
somehow,
physically and mentally
the beginning,
it becomes life
as you know it.

Death
as you know it
slowly
creeping into your life,

with the callous hardening
or draining of compassion
and capacity to feel love.

If the actual combat is intermittent
and allows you to recuperate
somewhat,
to regain some perspective
of reality,
there can be some semblance
of a normal life
and living.

But if it is steady,
ever present,
in your face,
foul smelling,
gory, gruesome and grim,
you become altered.

Hardened
like virgin skin,
callous enough with exposure
to hard work.

You become less hesitant
to be there,
to join the fight.

Then,
you become enthusiastic,
at least to the point
of getting busy
and getting it done.

But if this keeps up
it becomes common
and normal.

It becomes more difficult
to take it as seriously

as you should,

the distraction
of the sanctity of life,
the brutal transformation
of living beings into compost.

Life becomes cheap.
The dance becomes game-like
with no real dues to pay,
a fantasy of nightmares,
dreamless sleep
and cold blood.

They're dead.
They no longer touch your heart
or terrorize your mind.

Your senses are dull
and unable to appreciate the light touch.
Even children
are like young wild animals,
maybe not to be eaten
but fair game nonetheless.

And with a hard heart
and a cloaked mind
and spirit,
life becomes so cheap
that you no longer value your own.

Killing becomes just a way of relating
in some perverse,
diabolical way.

Violent emotions
are taken to the limit
without morals
or regard.

And this slow,

stealthful
vine wraps around your body.
Slowly moving about your legs
and trunk
squeezing the life
out of your heart,
compressing your soul
to near extinction.

You suddenly find yourself
overgrown
and threatened
to be compost
for the jungle as well.

The real horror
of violence
is that life becomes so cheap
that even yours is worthless.

Worthless to the world,
to those who would love you,
to your friends
or lovers
and worst of all
to you.

It isn't fair.
It isn't right.
But it is as real
as death itself.

There is no illusion
of heaven
or hell,
no dreams
or expectations
of willing virgins
awaiting you in paradise.

There is no comfort

or end to your difficult
or trying
existence.

You have nothing
to give,
nothing to lose.
You become nothing
that matters
even to yourself.

When life
becomes that cheap
it is no longer living.
It is death
and slow decay.

If you should
somehow
find yourself
washed up on the shore
of battle,
alive
in some fashion,
the heart beating,
the eyes seeing something
and lungs still taking in air,
it may be possible
to crawl away.

And if it is possible
to be somewhere more sane
and safe
feeling may
slowly,
ever so slowly,
drift back
into your fingertips
and bones.

It depends if the baggage

you bring home
is filled with blood and bones,
tears or just regret.

Your senses
may pick up hints
of beauty
instead of danger.

Your heart
may pump warm blood
through your veins,
again
not antifreeze.

Yes,
it is possible.
You may survive
and return to life.

Your limbs
may thaw out.
Your brain rise up
out of the morning fog
and your soul
embrace life.

Maybe.

Even horrific
physical wounds
can scar up
and heal
in some fashion.

The soul,
on the other hand,
is both more resilient
and vulnerable.

It's healing is torturous

but there is always the possibility
of regeneration
through all-encompassing love.

Yes,
it is possible
to come back to life
sometime,
for some people.

There will be no gods
to save you,
no saints
to pray to
for intervention,
no help
or relief
from those
that sent you.

There'll be no deals
on the Price is Right,
no sweet "thank you's"
or lottery surprise.

There'll be no "I'm sorry's."

It will just be
you,
left to your own destruction
or salvation.